FINGERPICKING
JAZZ STANDARDS

ISBN 978-1-4234-1653-1

HAL•LEONARD®
CORPORATION
7777 W. BLUEMOUND RD. P.O. BOX 13819 MILWAUKEE, WI 53213

Visit Hal Leonard Online at
www.halleonard.com

INTRODUCTION TO FINGERSTYLE GUITAR

Fingerstyle (a.k.a. fingerpicking) is a guitar technique that means you literally pick the strings with your right-hand fingers and thumb. This contrasts with the conventional technique of strumming and playing single notes with a pick (a.k.a. flatpicking). For fingerpicking, you can use any type of guitar: acoustic steel-string, nylon-string classical, or electric.

THE RIGHT HAND

The most common right-hand position is shown here.

Use a high wrist; arch your palm as if you were holding a ping-pong ball. Keep the thumb outside and away from the fingers, and let the fingers do the work rather than lifting your whole hand.

The thumb generally plucks the bottom strings with downstrokes on the left side of the thumb and thumbnail. The other fingers pluck the higher strings using upstrokes with the fleshy tip of the fingers and fingernails. The thumb and fingers should pluck one string per stroke and not brush over several strings.

Another picking option you may choose to use is called hybrid picking (a.k.a. plectrum-style fingerpicking). Here, the pick is usually held between the thumb and first finger, and the three remaining fingers are assigned to pluck the higher strings.

THE LEFT HAND

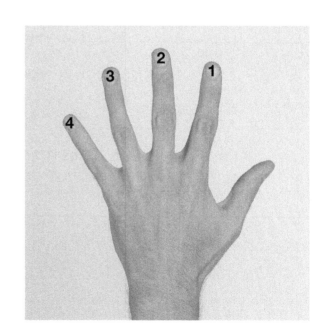

The left-hand fingers are numbered 1 through 4.

Be sure to keep your fingers arched, with each joint bent; if they flatten out across the strings, they will deaden the sound when you fingerpick. As a general rule, let the strings ring as long as possible when playing fingerstyle.

Can't Help Lovin' Dat Man

from SHOW BOAT

Lyrics by Oscar Hammerstein II
Music by Jerome Kern

mine. _____

When he goes a -

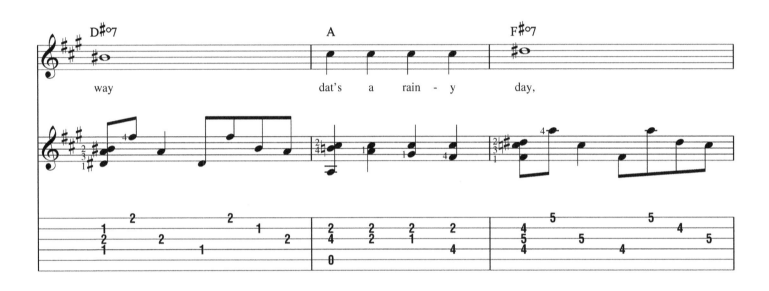

way   dat's a rain - y day,

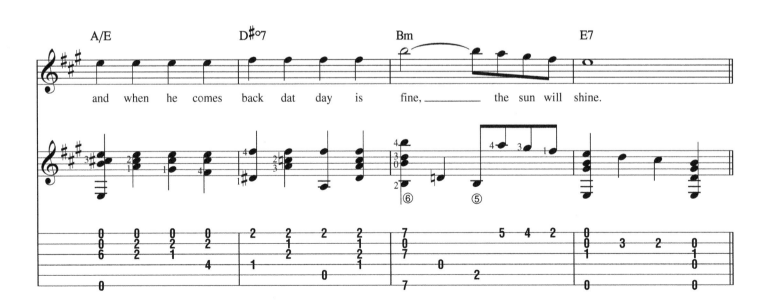

and when he comes back dat day is fine, _____ the sun will shine.

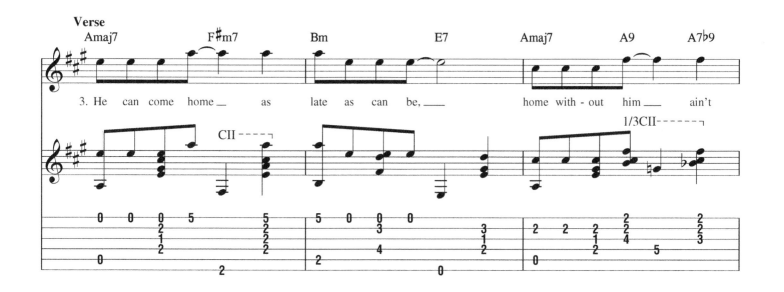

Verse

3. He can come home ___ as late as can be, ___ home with-out him ___ ain't

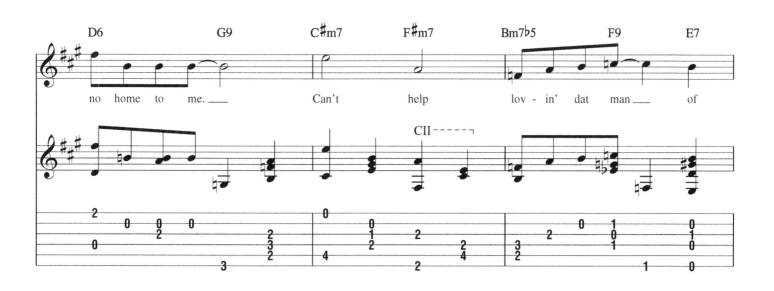

no home to me. ___ Can't help lov-in' dat man ___ of

mine. ___

Autumn in New York

Words and Music by Vernon Duke

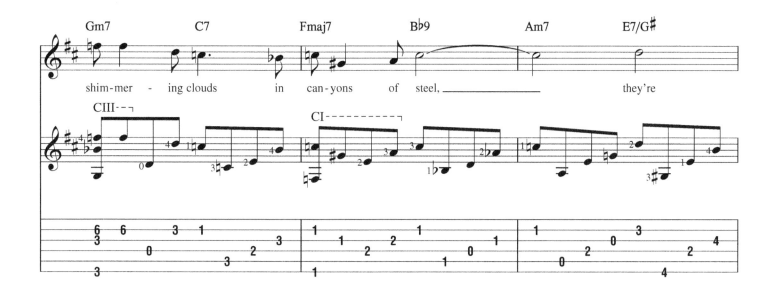

shim-mer - ing clouds in can-yons of steel, _____ they're

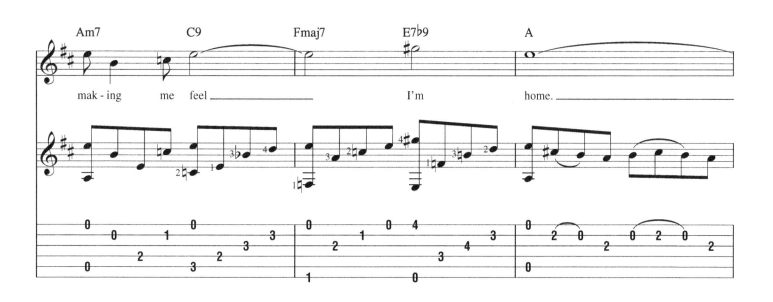

mak - ing me feel _____ I'm home. _____

_____ It's au-tumn in New York _____ that brings the prom-ise of

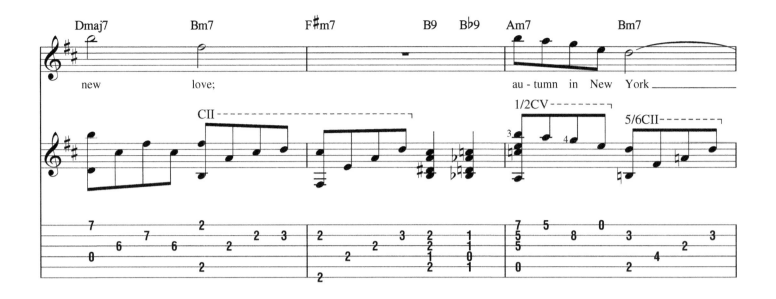

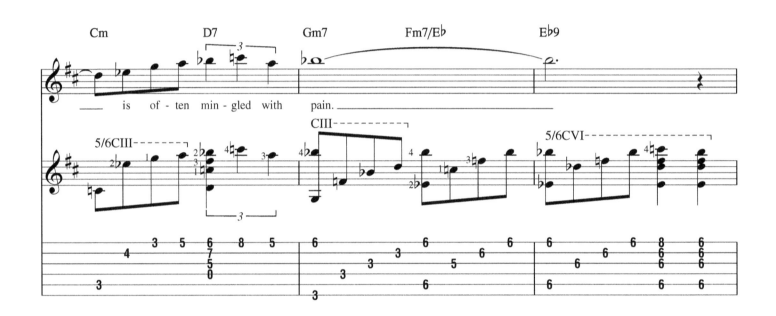

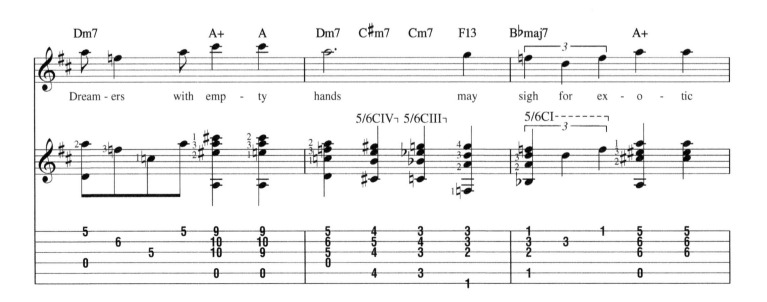

lands; it's au-tumn in New York, _____ it's good to live it a-

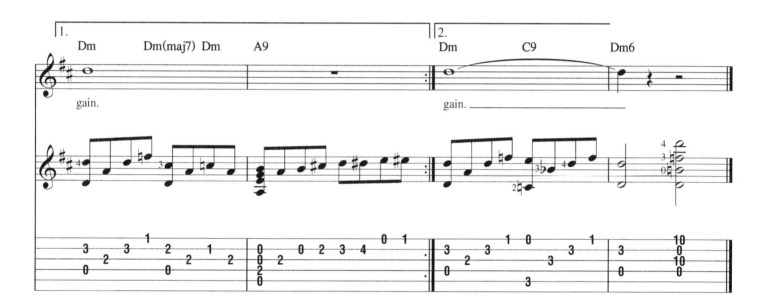

gain. gain. _____

Additional Lyrics

2. Autumn in New York,
   The gleaming rooftops at sundown.
   Autumn in New York,
   It lifts you up when you're rundown.

   Jaded roués and gay divorcees
   Who lunch at the Ritz
   Will tell you that "it's divine!"

   This autumn in New York
   Transforms the slums into Mayfair;
   Autumn in New York,
   You'll need no castles in Spain.

   Lovers that bless the dark
   On benches in Central Park
   Greet autumn in New York;
   It's good to live it again.

Body and Soul

Words by Edward Heyman, Robert Sour and Frank Eyton
Music by John Green

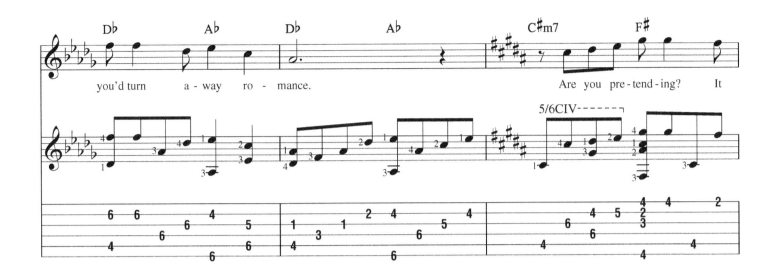

you'd turn a - way ro - mance. Are you pre - tend - ing? It

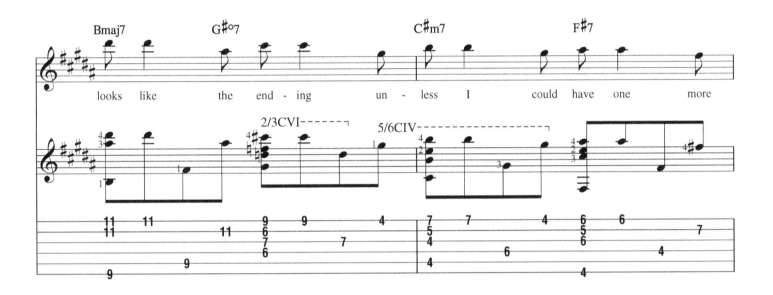

looks like the end - ing un - less I could have one more

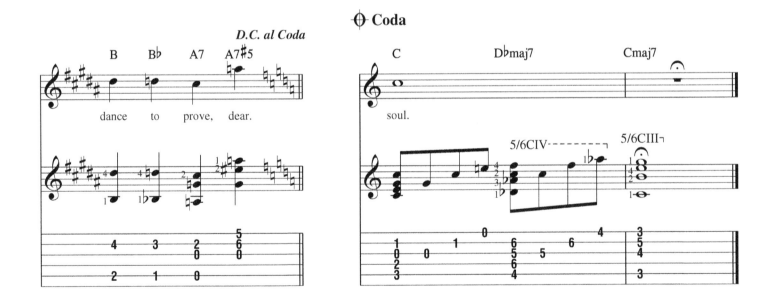

D.C. al Coda

dance to prove, dear.

⊕ Coda

soul.

Additional Lyrics

2. I spend my days in longing
   And wond'ring why it's me you're wronging.
   I tell you I mean it,
   I'm all for you, body and soul.

3. My life a wreck you're making.
   You know I'm yours for just the taking.
   I'd gladly surrender
   Myself to you, body and soul.

Easy Living

Theme from the Paramount Picture EASY LIVING

Words and Music by Leo Robin and Ralph Rainger

A Fine Romance

from SWING TIME

Words by Dorothy Fields
Music by Jerome Kern

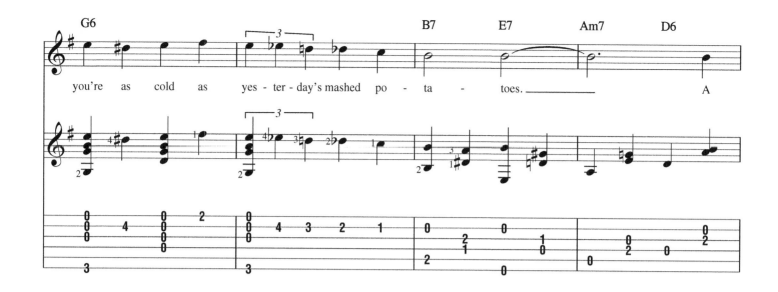

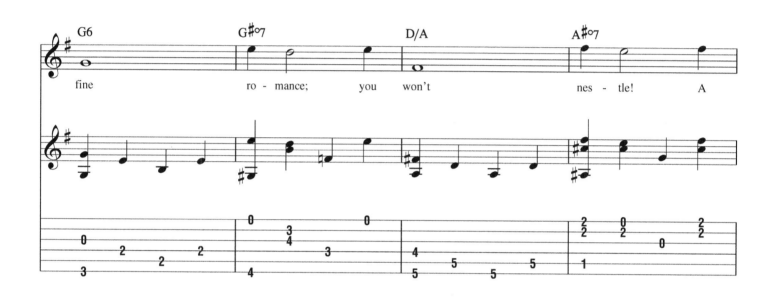

Additional Lyrics

2. A fine romance, my good fellow!
You take romance, I'll take Jell-O!
You're calmer than the seals in the Arctic Ocean;
At least they flap their fins to express emotion.

A fine romance, with no quarrels,
With no insults, and all morals!
I've never mussed the crease in your blue serge pants;
I never get the chance.
This is a fine romance!

Have You Met Miss Jones?

from I'D RATHER BE RIGHT

Words by Lorenz Hart
Music by Richard Rodgers

1. "Have you met Miss Jones?" some-one said as we shook hands. She was just Miss Jones to me.

2. Then I said, "Miss Jones, you're a girl who un-der-stands I'm a man who must be free." And all at once I lost my

It Could Happen to You

from the Paramount Picture AND THE ANGELS SING

Words by Johnny Burke
Music by James Van Heusen

Drop D tuning:
(low to high) D-A-D-G-B-E

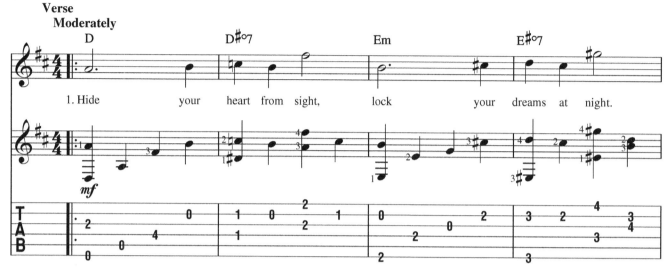

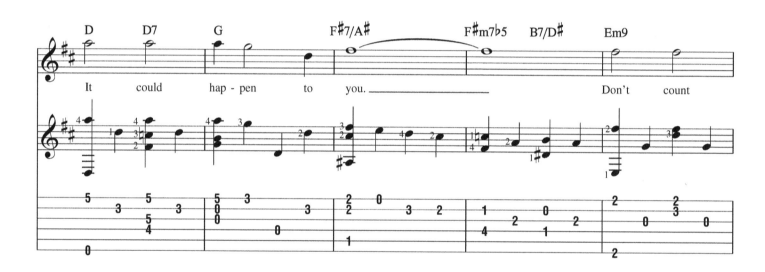

I'm Beginning to See the Light

Words and Music by Don George, Johnny Hodges, Duke Ellington and Harry James

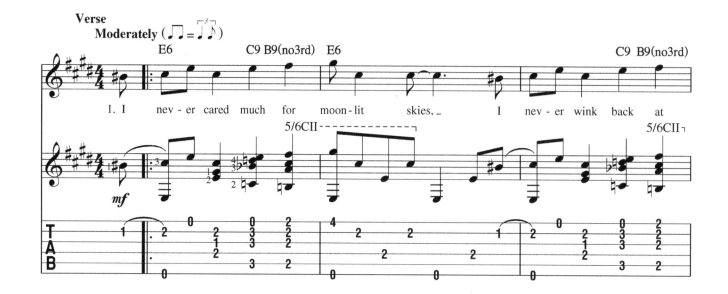

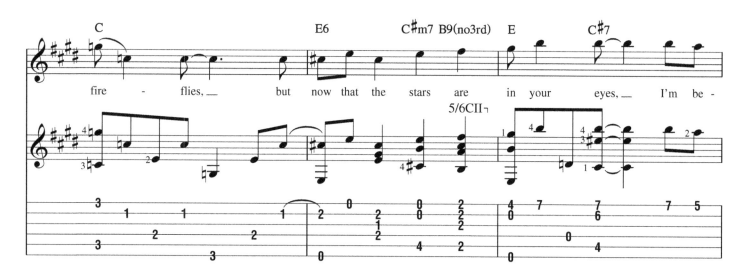

My Romance

from JUMBO

Words by Lorenz Hart
Music by Richard Rodgers

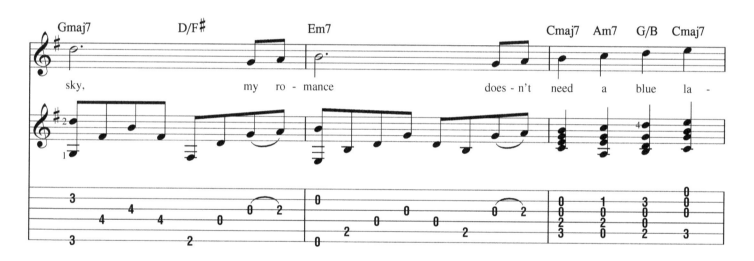

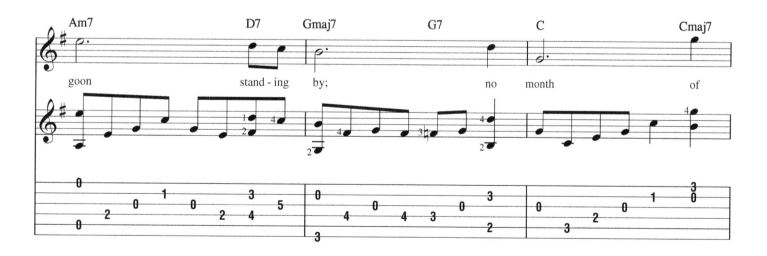

Stella by Starlight

from the Paramount Picture THE UNINVITED

Words by Ned Washington
Music by Victor Young

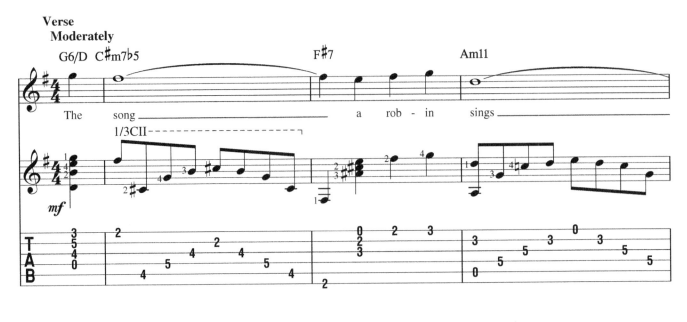

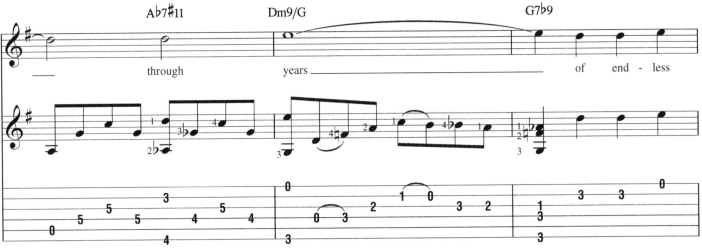

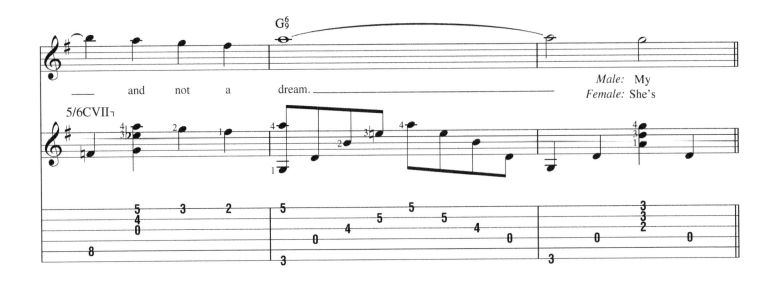

Tangerine

from the Paramount Picture THE FLEET'S IN

Words by Johnny Mercer
Music by Victor Schertzinger

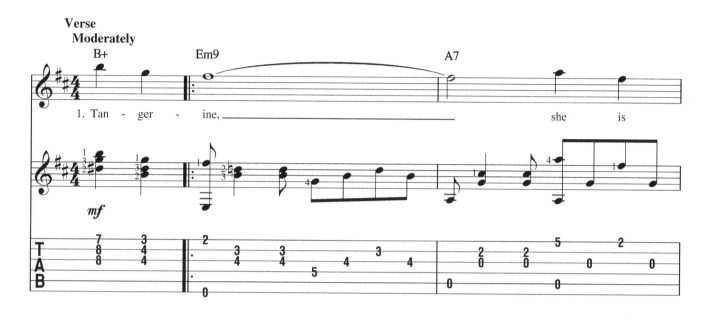

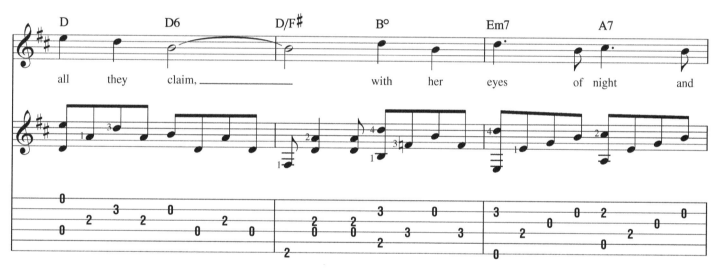

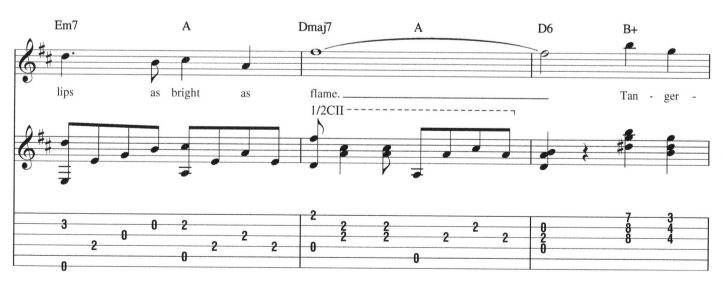

The Very Thought of You

Words and Music by Ray Noble

The Way You Look Tonight

from SWING TIME

Words by Dorothy Fields
Music by Jerome Kern

When Sunny Gets Blue

Lyric by Jack Segal
Music by Marvin Fisher

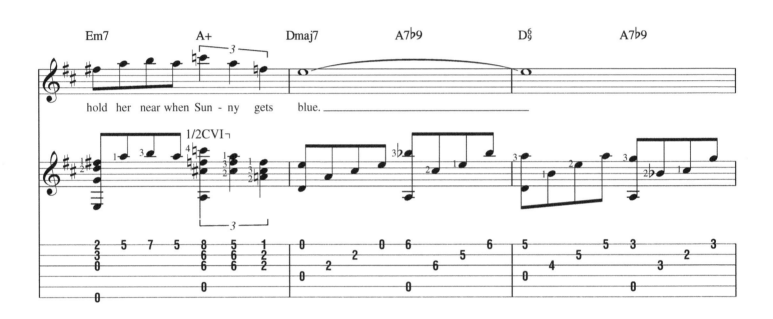

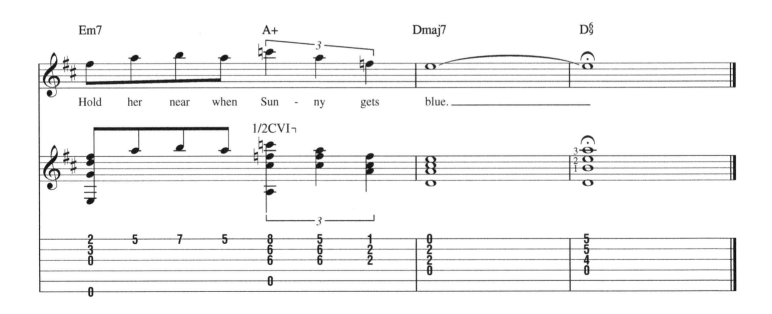

Yesterdays

from ROBERTA
from LOVELY TO LOOK AT

Words by Otto Harbach
Music by Jerome Kern

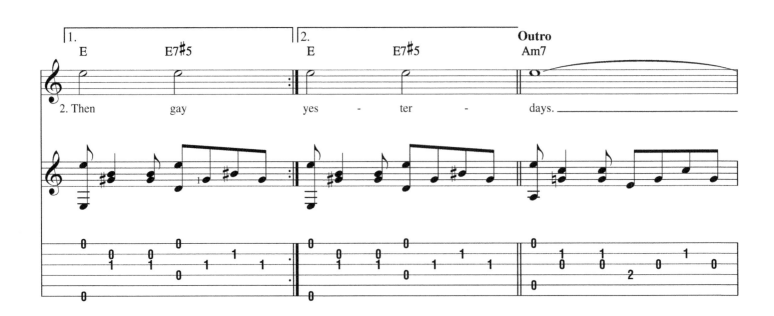

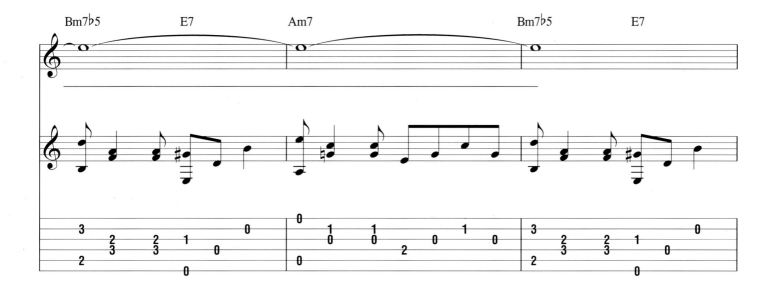

Additional Lyrics

2. Then gay youth was mine,
   Truth was mine.
   Joyous, free and flaming life,
   Forsooth, was mine.
   Sad am I, glad am I,
   For today I'm dreaming of yesterdays.

FINGERPICKING GUITAR BOOKS

Hone your fingerpicking skills with these great songbooks featuring solo guitar arrangements in standard notation and tablature. The arrangements in these books are carefully written for intermediate-level guitarists. Each song combines melody and harmony in one superb guitar fingerpicking arrangement. Each book also includes an introduction to basic fingerstyle guitar.

    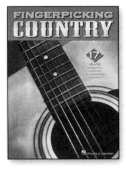 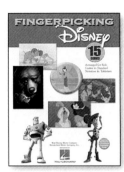

Fingerpicking Acoustic
00699614 15 songs......................$14.99

Fingerpicking Acoustic Classics
00160211 15 songs......................$16.99

Fingerpicking Acoustic Hits
00160202 15 songs......................$15.99

Fingerpicking Acoustic Rock
00699764 14 songs......................$16.99

Fingerpicking Ballads
00699717 15 songs......................$15.99

Fingerpicking Beatles
00699049 30 songs......................$24.99

Fingerpicking Beethoven
00702390 15 pieces....................$10.99

Fingerpicking Blues
00701277 15 songs $12.99

**Fingerpicking
Broadway Favorites**
00699843 15 songs........................$9.99

Fingerpicking Broadway Hits
00699838 15 songs........................$7.99

Fingerpicking Campfire
00275964 15 songs......................$14.99

Fingerpicking Celtic Folk
00701148 15 songs......................$12.99

Fingerpicking Children's Songs
00699712 15 songs........................$9.99

Fingerpicking Christian
00701076 15 songs......................$12.99

Fingerpicking Christmas
00699599 20 carols.....................$12.99

**Fingerpicking
Christmas Classics**
00701695 15 songs........................$7.99

Fingerpicking Christmas Songs
00171333 15 songs......................$10.99

Fingerpicking Classical
00699620 15 pieces....................$10.99

Fingerpicking Country
00699687 17 songs......................$12.99

Fingerpicking Disney
00699711 15 songs......................$17.99

**Fingerpicking
Early Jazz Standards**
00276565 15 songs $14.99

Fingerpicking Duke Ellington
00699845 15 songs........................$9.99

Fingerpicking Enya
00701161 15 songs......................$16.99

Fingerpicking Film Score Music
00160143 15 songs......................$15.99

Fingerpicking Gospel
00701059 15 songs........................$9.99

Fingerpicking Hit Songs
00160195 15 songs......................$12.99

Fingerpicking Hymns
00699688 15 hymns $12.99

Fingerpicking Irish Songs
00701965 15 songs......................$10.99

Fingerpicking Italian Songs
00159778 15 songs......................$12.99

Fingerpicking Jazz Favorites
00699844 15 songs......................$14.99

Fingerpicking Jazz Standards
00699840 15 songs......................$12.99

Fingerpicking Elton John
00237495 15 songs......................$15.99

Fingerpicking Latin Favorites
00699842 15 songs......................$12.99

Fingerpicking Latin Standards
00699837 15 songs......................$17.99

Fingerpicking Love Songs
00699841 15 songs......................$14.99

Fingerpicking Love Standards
00699836 15 songs $9.99

Fingerpicking Lullabyes
00701276 16 songs........................$9.99

Fingerpicking Movie Music
00699919 15 songs......................$14.99

Fingerpicking Mozart
00699794 15 pieces....................$10.99

Fingerpicking Pop
00699615 15 songs......................$14.99

Fingerpicking Popular Hits
00139079 14 songs......................$12.99

Fingerpicking Praise
00699714 15 songs......................$14.99

Fingerpicking Rock
00699716 15 songs......................$14.99

Fingerpicking Standards
00699613 17 songs......................$15.99

Fingerpicking Worship
00700554 15 songs......................$15.99

**Fingerpicking Neil Young –
Greatest Hits**
00700134 16 songs......................$17.99

Fingerpicking Yuletide
00699654 16 songs......................$12.99

  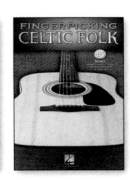